Annual Report on Vital Signs Monitoring Of Wolf (*Canis lupus*) Distribution and Abundance in Yukon-Charley Rivers National Preserve, Central Alaska Network: 2009 Report

Natural Resource Technical Report NPS/CAKN/NRTR—2009/228

John Burch
National Park Service
Yukon-Charley Rivers National Preserve
4175 Geist Road
Fairbanks, AK 99709
John_Burch@NPS.GOV

July 2009

U.S. Department of the Interior
National Park Service
Natural Resource Program Center
Fort Collins, Colorado

The National Park Service, Natural Resource Program Center publishes a range of reports that address natural resource topics of interest and applicability to a broad audience in the National Park Service and others in natural resource management, including scientists, conservation and environmental constituencies, and the public.

The Natural Resource Report Series is used to disseminate high-priority, current natural resource management information with managerial application. The series targets a general, diverse audience, and may contain NPS policy considerations or address sensitive issues of management applicability.

All manuscripts in the series receive the appropriate level of peer review to ensure that the information is scientifically credible, technically accurate, appropriately written for the intended audience, and designed and published in a professional manner.

This report received informal peer review by subject-matter experts who were not directly involved in the collection, analysis, or reporting of the data. Data in this report were collected and analyzed using methods based on established, peer-reviewed protocols and were analyzed and interpreted within the guidelines of the protocols.

Views, statements, findings, conclusions, recommendations, and data in this report are those of the author(s) and do not necessarily reflect views and policies of the National Park Service, U.S. Department of the Interior. Mention of trade names or commercial products does not constitute endorsement or recommendation for use by the National Park Service.

This report is available from The National Park Service, Central Alaska Network website (http://science.nature.nps.gov/im/units/cakn) and the Natural Resource Publications Management website (http://www.nature.nps.gov/publications/NRPM).

Please cite this publication as:

Burch, J. 2009. Annual report on vital signs monitoring of wolf (*Canis lupus*) distribution and abundance in Yukon-Charley Rivers National Preserve, Central Alaska Network: 2009 report. Natural Resource Technical Report NPS/CAKN/NRTR— 2009/228. National Park Service, Fort Collins, Colorado.

NPS 191/100168, July 2009.

Contents

Figures

Figures (continued)

Executive Summary

- Wolf populations have been monitored in Yukon-Charley Rivers National Preserve (YUCH) from March 1993 to present (Burch 2002, Burch 2006, Burch 2007, Burch 2008). Beginning October 2005 the project was incorporated into CAKN Vital signs monitoring program.

- Wolves throughout the greater Yukon-Charley Rivers area are targeted for monitoring of abundance and distribution. This past winter, wolf captures were conducted in November 2008 and February 2009. Monitoring radiocollared packs via radio telemetry flights will occur throughout the year with a concentrated period of flights each year in March – April and again in September – October. All field work is conducted using 1 or 2 biologists and 1 - 3 pilots.

- In winter 08-09, 11 more wolves in 6 packs were captured and collared. We had good snow conditions for searching for uncollared packs in 5 areas in February 2009, yet only the 70 Mile Pack was re-found after loosing radio contact earlier in the year. Tracks of 6 were seen in the Webber Creek area, but we could not find the wolves. Old tracks of 2 or 3 wolves were found in the Hard Luck area. In the remaining 2 areas no old tracks were seen indicating that wolf packs may not exist in areas where they once did. At least 3 areas where packs once lived remain without collared wolves and we hope to find and capture wolves from these packs in winter 09-10.

- The Fall 2008 wolf density (5.86 wolves/1000 km^2) marked the highest wolf density measured in Yuch since 1993, however this was followed by the largest fall to spring drop in the population to a spring 2009 density of 2.41 wolves/1000 km^2 similar to spring 2008.

- Fall 2008 mean pack size was 8.3 wolves/ pack.

- Fall 2008 average litter size was 4.1 pups/ pack.

- At least six wolves were trapped or snared within YUCH in winter 2008-09 that we know of. ADF&G harvest data is not yet available for 07-08, or 08-09.

- No substantial changes in protocol are anticipated for the upcoming field season for biological year 09-10 (May 1, 2009 – April 30, 2010).

Key Words

Yukon-Charley Rivers National Preserve, wolves, *Canis lupus*, radiotelemetry, population dynamics, density estimation.

Acknowledgments

This study was funded by U.S. National Park Service Central Alaska Network and Yukon-Charley Rivers National Preserve, Alaska. The skilled and safe aircraft support provided during the study by S. Hamilton, D. Miller, R. Swisher, and T. Cambier is always much appreciated. None of the work gets done without the pilots, they are there for every observation, data point, and capture, and are often the unsung heroes of most wildlife survey work throughout Alaska. Tom Meier and David James reviewed the report and made several helpful comments.

Introduction

CAKN has adopted a holistic view of network ecosystems and will track the major physical drivers of ecosystem change and responses of the two major components of the biota, plants and animals. Thus, CAKN has identified Fauna Distribution and Abundance as one of its top three vital signs. In general, CAKN wants to know where fauna are distributed across the landscape and to track changes in both their distribution and abundance. The Fauna Distribution and Abundance vital sign includes monitoring efforts for a suite of vertebrate species spanning the significant elevation gradient found in CAKN parks, and also including species of specific interest within each park. Wolves (*Canis lupus*), occur in all three network parks and are one of six keystone large mammal species in interior Alaska. Wolves are of great importance to people from both consumptive and non-consumptive viewpoints, and to the ecosystem as a whole. From a monitoring standpoint, wolves are considered to be good indicators of long-term habitat change within park ecosystems because they depend on healthy populations of large ungulate prey, which in turn respond to vegetation, weather and other habitat patterns across the entire landscape (Mech and Peterson 2003, Fuller et al. 2003). As a top predator, wolves can play a key role in influencing ungulate populations, and as a result may influence vegetation patterns (Miller et al. 2001, Ripple and Beschta 2003). The effects of wolves on ungulate populations may be important determinants of ungulate availability for subsistence harvest on NPS Park and Preserve lands in Alaska, and harvest by the general public on NPS Preserve lands (National Park Service 2001).

Wolves are a species specifically identified in the enabling legislation and management objectives of all three CAKN parks (U. S. Congress 1980). Wolves are important to park visitors because of the unique opportunities to view or hear wolves in Alaskan parks. While the primary objectives of wolf monitoring will be to track the distribution and abundance of wolves, a variety of accessory data will be obtained in the monitoring process that are likely to be valuable for wildlife management and research. The body of data on wolf populations in Alaska parks is of great value in developing scientific models of predator/prey systems. In heavily visited portions of the parks, managers may want to know the locations of active wolf dens and rendezvous sites so that they can be protected from disturbance. When intensive wolf harvest or wolf control take place near parks, it is important to know home range boundaries and travel patterns of wolf packs utilizing park lands. These data are used to determine and possibly mitigate impacts of wolf control activities outside the parks. Data on the genetic and morphological characteristics of wolves, obtained as a sidelight to wolf capture, are important in evaluating long-term changes in wolf populations in Alaska.

Measurable Objectives

- Locate non-radiocollared wolf packs utilizing Preserve lands by snow tracking.
- Capture and radio-collar 1 -3 individuals in each wolf pack identified in the study area.
- Determine the demography (numbers, colors, age structure) of wolf packs using Preserve lands.
- Obtain morphological measurements from captured wolves.
- Obtain genotypic data (mitochondrial and microsatellite DNA) from captured wolves.
- Obtain immunological (disease exposure) data from captured wolves.
- Define home ranges of collared wolf packs via GPS collar data and aerial telemetry.
- Determine pack size for each collared pack in fall (early winter) and spring (late winter) each biological year (May 1 – April 30).
- Define the mosaic of wolf home ranges (population area) for estimating biannual wolf densities (fall and spring of each biological year).
- Perform annual capture efforts to maintain coverage of radio collars in the population.
- Detect pack extinction and pack formation events in the population.
- Detect changes in wolf density over time
- Detect changes in wolf pack size over time
- Detect changes in wolf home range size over time.
- Detect changes in the morphological, immunological, and genetic makeup of the wolf population over time.

Methods and Materials

Methods followed the wolf monitoring protocol (Meier and Burch 2004) and include aerial radio telemetry, the use of GPS collars, and direct observation as primary techniques. Radiotelemetry and GPS provide the most effective way to identify and monitor individual packs and populations of wolves as well as to monitor natality, recruitment, causes and rates of mortality and dispersal, and predator – prey relationships (Mech et. al. 1998, Mech and Barber 2002).

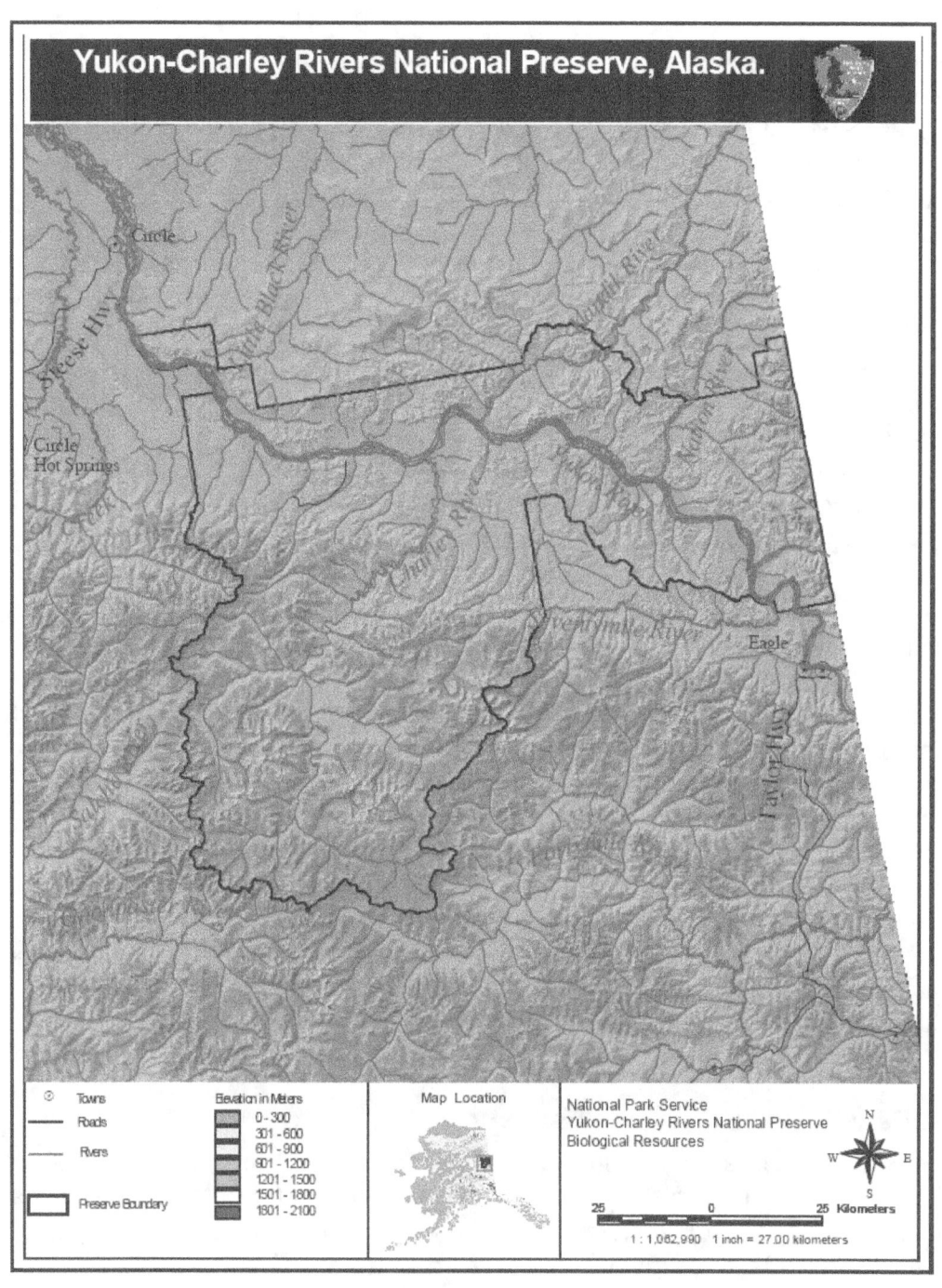

Figure 1. Wolf monitoring study area, Yukon-Charley Rivers National Preserve.

Results and Discussion

Captures and Radio Telemetry

During November 2008 and February 2009, 11 wolves were captured and radio-collared in or near YUCH, 3 of which were recaptures. Sex and age composition of captured wolves included 3 adult males, 3 male pups, 3 adult females, and 2 yearling females. The capture sample is biased toward adult wolves as breeding adult wolves were specifically targeted because they are much less likely to disperse. Colors of captured wolves varied widely from black to 'blue' (silver gray) to various shades of gray to white. Over the history of the project weights of captured males ranged from 70-148 lbs., (32-67 kg) averaging 108 lbs (49 kg), captured females ranged from 57-130 lbs. (26–59 kg) and averaged 90 lbs (41 kg).

Home range Sizes and Movements

Previous home range sizes for individual Preserve packs varied from $268 - 7067$ km^2. Annual means ranged from 1639 to 3253 km^2 with a grand mean of 2295 km^2, which is larger than found in most other wolf studies (Figures 2-6) (Burch 2002). With the advent of GPS collars, the annual number of locations per pack has increased nearly 10 fold and with it an increase in individual home range size (Burch et al. 2005). Home range of packs containing one GPS collar were more than 35% larger than those found using conventional aerial telemetry (Figure 7).

In past years, home range size was measured for each radiomarked pack where more than 20 locations were available in a 2 year time block. This was an attempt to overcome the problem of home range size being dependent on the sample size of locations (when calculated using Minimum Convex Polygons (MCP)). Even with this doubling of sample size the relationship still holds ($r^2 = 19.4, P = 0.00017, n = 67$) (Figure 8) and home range size was still dependent on the number of locations (White and Garrott 1990). With the advent of GPS collars, 1 biological year of locations is used, but the problem of home range size being dependent on sample size looks like it may still exist even with 300 locations per year, although the effect is much smaller. In the upcoming year we are looking into kernel estimates and bootstrapping as a possible solution to this problem (Worton 1989).

Pack Sizes, Density and Population Estimate

Fall mean pack sizes increased from 4.3 in 1993 to a maximum of 9.1 in 1999, with an overall average of 7.1 (Figure 10). The wolf population in the area is currently fluctuating widely and is likely responding to changes in the accessibility and vulnerability to predation of Fortymile Caribou. From $1993 - 2001$ the overall increasing trend in mean pack size was significant ($r^2=0.59, P=0.015$), however from 2002 on it levels out and then drops in 2005 (Figure 10). Wolf densities follow the same trends as mean pack sizes (Figures 11 & 12). Most recently, the population hit an all time low density of 1.6 wolves/1000 km^2 in spring 2007, then rebounded to almost 2.5 in spring 2008. The fall 2008 wolf density estimate was the highest calculated since the study began in 1993 at 5.86 wolves/1000 km2. This was followed by the largest drop in population size to a spring 2009 density of 2.41 wolves/1000 km^2. Fall densities are measured when pack size is at its highest and densities are at the greatest for the biological year and follow the same overall trend pattern as Mean pack size and Spring densities (Figure 11). Pack sizes are actually greater right after pups are born in May. However, we cannot reliably count all the pups from airplanes in all the packs until September or October when the pups are traveling consistently with the rest of the pack and there might be some snow on the ground to increase sightability.

Figure 2. **Spring 2009** map of individual pack home ranges, pack counts, and density calculation. Minimum convex polygons are used to delineate pack home ranges.

BioYear 0809, May 1, 2008 - April 30, 2009
Home Range Data, May 1, 2008 - April 30, 2009
Fall, 2008 Wolf Density Estimate:

Density Calculation Date = 6/16/09
Fall 2008 Wolf Packs and Counts
1. Copper Mt = 7
2. Lost Creek = 8
3. Stirling Cr = 9
4. 70 mile = 9
5. Lower Charley = 9
6. Edwards = 6
7. Step Mt = 10
8. Black River = 1 (not included)

Total wolves = 58
Mean Pack Size = 8.29 (n=7)
Add 8% lone wolves = 63

Population Area = 9902 km2
Density = 5.86 wolves/1000 km2
Add 8% lone wolves = 6.36 wolves/1000 km2
Preserve Size = 10198 km2

Preserve Extrapolation = 60 wolves
Add 8% lone wolves = 65 wolves

Wolf Home Ranges

Wolf Population Area

Preserve Boundary

Wolf Control Area

Figure 3. **Fall 2008** map of individual pack home ranges, pack counts, and density calculation. Minimum convex polygons are used to delineate pack home ranges.

BioYear 0708, May 1, 2007 - April 30, 2008
Home Range Data, May 1, 2007 - April 30, 2008
Spring, 2008 Wolf Density Estimate:

Spring 2008 Wolf Packs and Counts
1. Copper Mt = 2
2. Crescent Cr = 0
3. Lost Creek = 9
4. Stirling Cr = 4
5. 70 mile = 9
6. Edwards = 3
7. Lower Charley = 4
8. Step Mt = 3
9. Black River = 2 (not included)

Total wolves = 34
Mean Pack Size = 4.0 (n=9)
Add 8% lone wolves = 37

Population Area = 13786 km2
Density = 2.47 wolves/1000 km2
Add 8% lone wolves = 2.68 wolves/1000 km2
Preserve Size = 10198 km2

Preserve Extrapolation = 25 wolves
Add 8% lone wolves = 27 wolves

☐ Wolf Home Ranges

☐ Wolf Population Area

☐ Preserve Boundary

Wolf Control Area

Figure 4. **Spring 2008** map of individual pack home ranges, pack counts, and density calculation. Minimum convex polygons are used to delineate pack home ranges.

Fall 2007 Wolf Packs and Counts
1. Copper Mt = 5
2. Crescent Cr = 6
3. Lost Creek = 9
4. Stirling Cr = 7
5. 70 mile = 13
6. Edwards = 3
7. Lower Charley = 4
8. Step Mt = 2
9. Black River = 3 (not included)

Total wolves = 49
Mean Pack Size = 5.8 (n=9)
Add 8% lone wolves = 53

Population Area = 13786 km2
Density = 3.55 wolves/1000 km2
Add 8% lone wolves = 3.84 wolves/1000 km2
Preserve Size = 10198 km2

Preserve Extrapolation = 36 wolves
Add 8% lone wolves = 39 wolves

Wolf Home Ranges

Wolf Population Area

Preserve Boundary

Wolf Control Area

BioYear 0708, May 1, 2007 - April 30, 2008
Home Range Data, May 1, 2007 - April 30, 2008
Fall, 2007 Wolf Density Estimate:

Figure 5. **Fall 2007** map of individual pack home ranges, pack counts, and density calculation for. Minimum convex polygons are used to delineate pack home ranges.

BioYear 0607, May 1 2006 - April 30, 2007
Fall, 2006 Wolf Density Estimate

Fall 2006 Wolf Packs and Counts
1. Copper Mt   = 5
2. Crescent Creek = 3
3. Puzzle Gultch   = 10
4. Sterling Cr   = ? (captured Feb 2006)
5. Hanna Cr   = 6
6. Andrew Cr   = 2
7. 70Mile   = 11
8. Edwards Cr   = 4
9. Step Mt   = 6
10. Upper Black   = 2

 Total Wolves = 49
 Mean Pack Size = 5.4 (n=9)
 Add 8% lone wolves = 53

Population Area = 14865 km2
Density = 3.30 wolves/1000 km2
Add 8% lone wolves = 3.57 wolves/1000 km2
Preserve Size = 10198 km2

Preserve estimate = 34 wolves
Add 8% lone wolves = 36 wolves

☐ Wolf Home Ranges

☐ Wolf Population Area

☐ Preserve Boundary

   Wolf Control Area starting 9/1/06

Figure 6. **Fall 2006** map of individual pack home ranges, pack counts, and density calculation for. Minimum convex polygons are used to delineate pack home ranges.

Figure 7. Wolf home ranges measured with GPS collars are over 35% larger on average than those from conventional aerial radiotelemetry (VHF) when measured over the same time period. Average GPS home range = 3322 km². Average VHF home Range = 1211 km². Not all home ranges depicted for clarity.

Figure 8. Wolf home range size vs. number of locations showing that home ranges calculated using minimum convex polygons are dependent on sample size of locations. Yukon-Charley Rivers National Preserve, Alaska, 1993 – 2005.

Figure 9. Map depicting the recent history and progression of wolf control boundaries relative to YUCH. UYTPCA (Upper Yukon Tanana Predator Control Area) = 48,550 km^2 (red line) has been in effect since Sept 2006.

Fall Mean Pack Sizes for Wolves in Yukon-Charley Rivers National Preserve

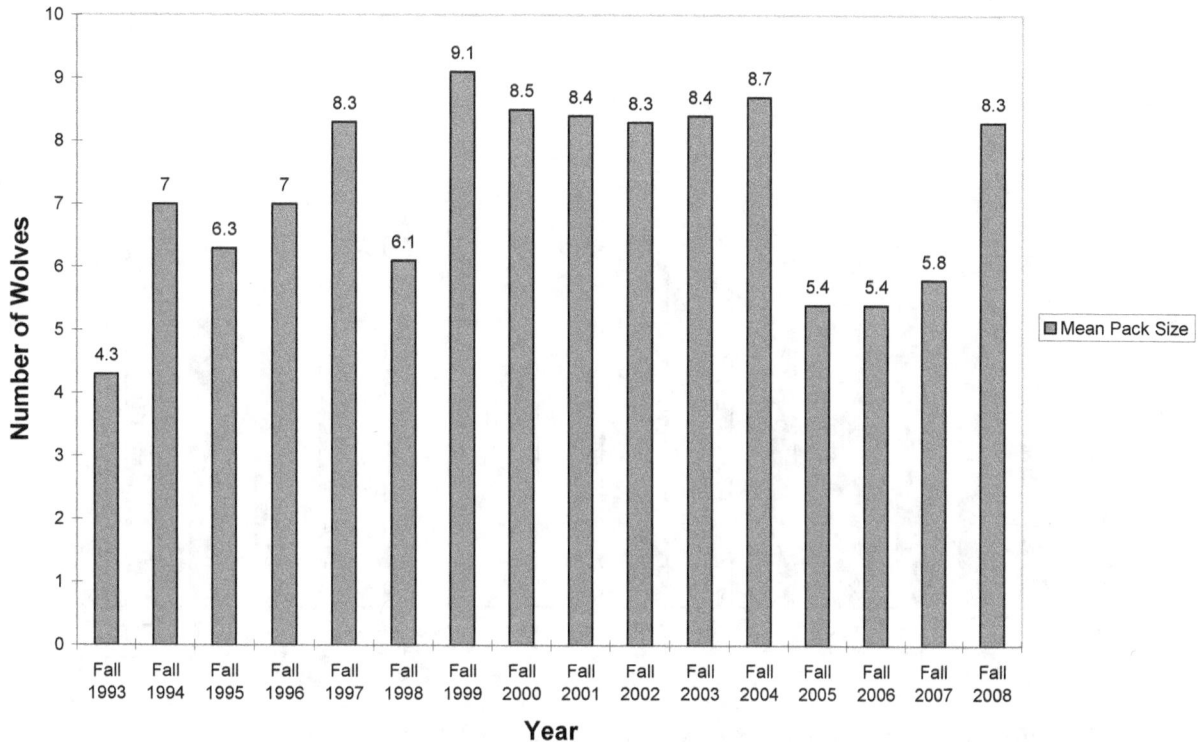

Figure 10. Trend in wolf population using mean pack size. Yukon-Charley Rivers National Preserve 1993 – 2008.

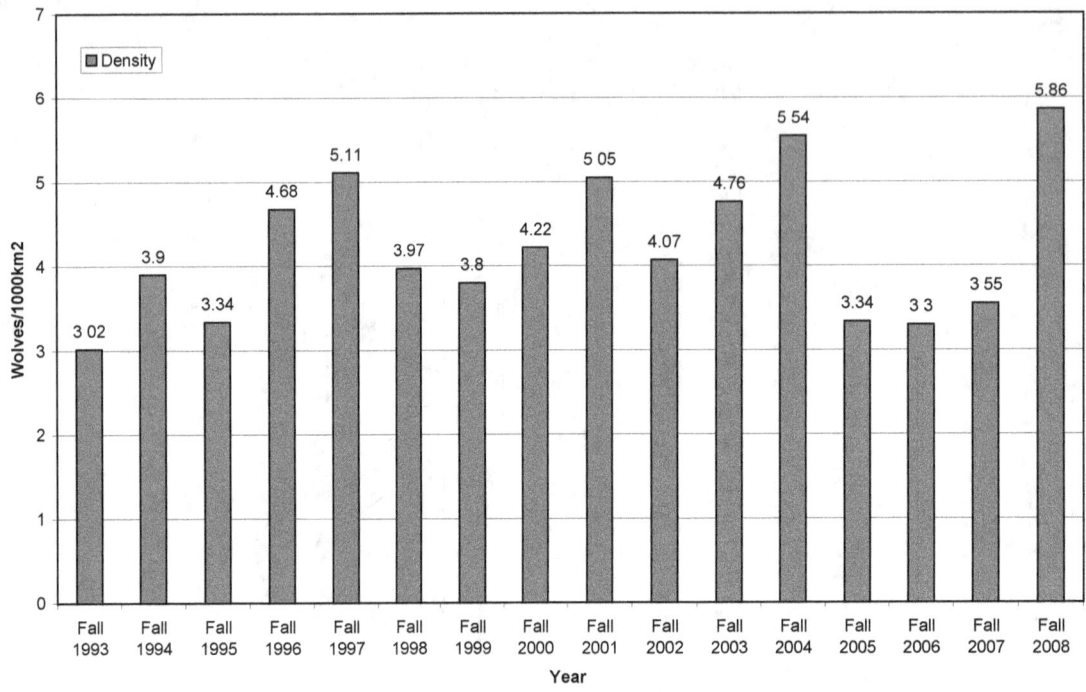

Figure 11. Fall wolf densities (wolves/1000 km^2) in YUCH 1993 – 2008.

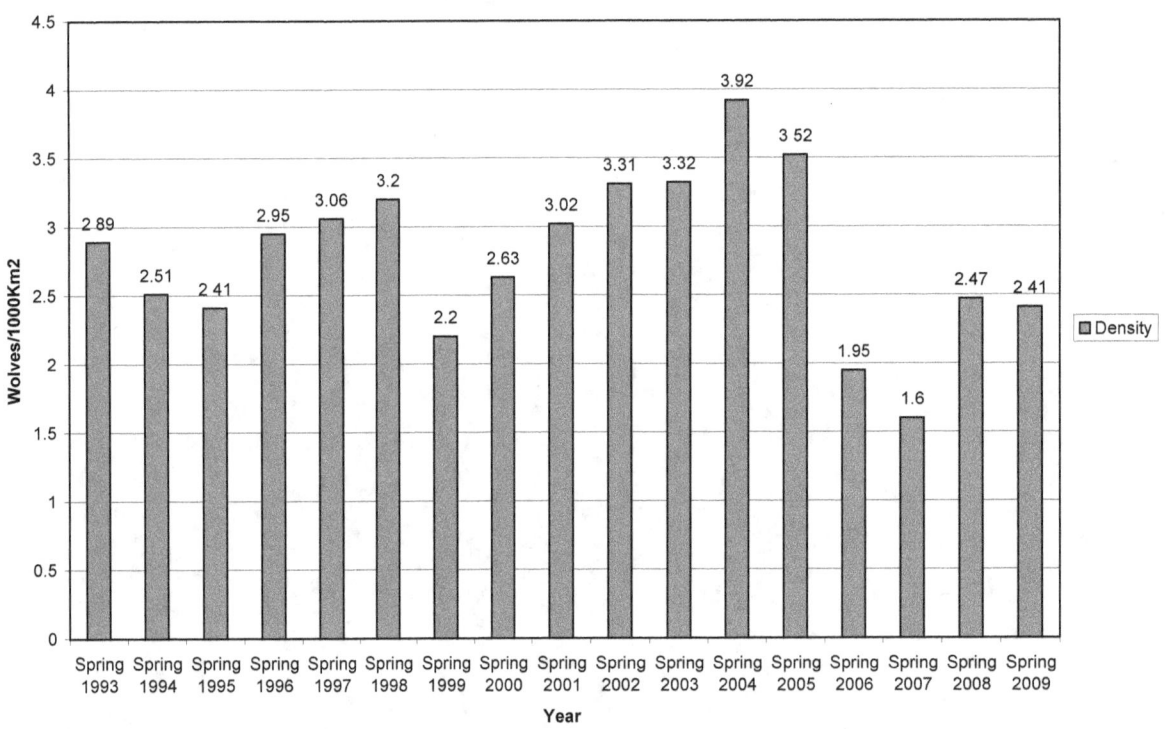

Figure 12 – Spring wolf densities (wolves/1000km^2) in YUCH, 1993 - 2009

Figure 13. Comparing fall wolf population (extrapolating fall densities to the YUCH Preserve boundary to estimate the number of wolves in the Preserve at any given time) with location counts.

Fortymile Caribou

In 1920 biologist Olaus Murie estimated the Forty Mile Caribou Herd (FCH) to number 568,000 caribou, and the herd ranged from Whitehorse, Yukon to the White Mountains north of Fairbanks (Murie 1935). It is difficult to know how accurate Murie's estimate was as he estimated how many caribou crossed a 1 mile stretch of the Steese Highway in one day and then multiplies that number for a forty mile stretch for 20 days, which is what was reported by others to be the place and time that the herd crossed the road (Murie 1935). In the 1930s the herd population dropped to an estimated 10,000 to 20,000 caribou. The cause of this dramatic decline is unknown but suspicions include overharvest, and food limitations due to range depletion and fires, or other wide spread phenomena. Predation was not considered a causal factor (Valkenburg et al 1994).

During the 1940s and 1950s the herd increased again to perhaps as many as 50,000. From an estimated 50,000 animals in 1963 the herd size dropped dramatically again to 6000 animals in 1973 and Fortymile caribou stopped crossing the Steese Highway. The cause of this decline was attributed to a combination of overharvest, deep snow conditions, and predation by wolves and bears. Starting in 1976, the herd began to increase slowly to over 22,000 by 1990 and was roughly stable at 22000 – 23000 through 1995 (Valkenburg et al 1994, Boertje and Gardner

1996). In 1994 the Fortymile Planning Team was formed and plans for wolf reductions and reduced human harvest on caribou were made. From 1995 through 2002, the herd grew to nearly 45,000 animals (Boertje and Gardner 1996, Jeff Gross, Tok area biologist, Pers. Comm.) where it remained roughly stable through 2006. The most recent photo census of June 2007 produced a population estimate of 38,364 (Jeff Gross, Tok area biologist, Pers. Comm.) (Figure 14). No photo census occurred in 2008 due to cool/rainy weather resulting in the caribou not grouping up enough to conduct the census. As of the writing of this report in June 2009 no information is available yet on the spring 2009 composition counts or photo census.

The drop in wolf numbers in 2005 – 2007 does not correlate well with the roughly stable caribou population during the same time (Figure 14). Low snowfall winters at this time may have allowed the caribou (and moose) to be less vulnerable to wolf predation, thereby causing an increase in wolf dispersal and natural mortality and a decrease in pup production and survival (Figure 15), culminating in a drop in the wolf population. Human Harvest levels at this time were lower than the 23 year annual average of about 7 wolves harvested within the Preserve (Figures 16 &17) and likely played no role in the drop in wolf numbers.

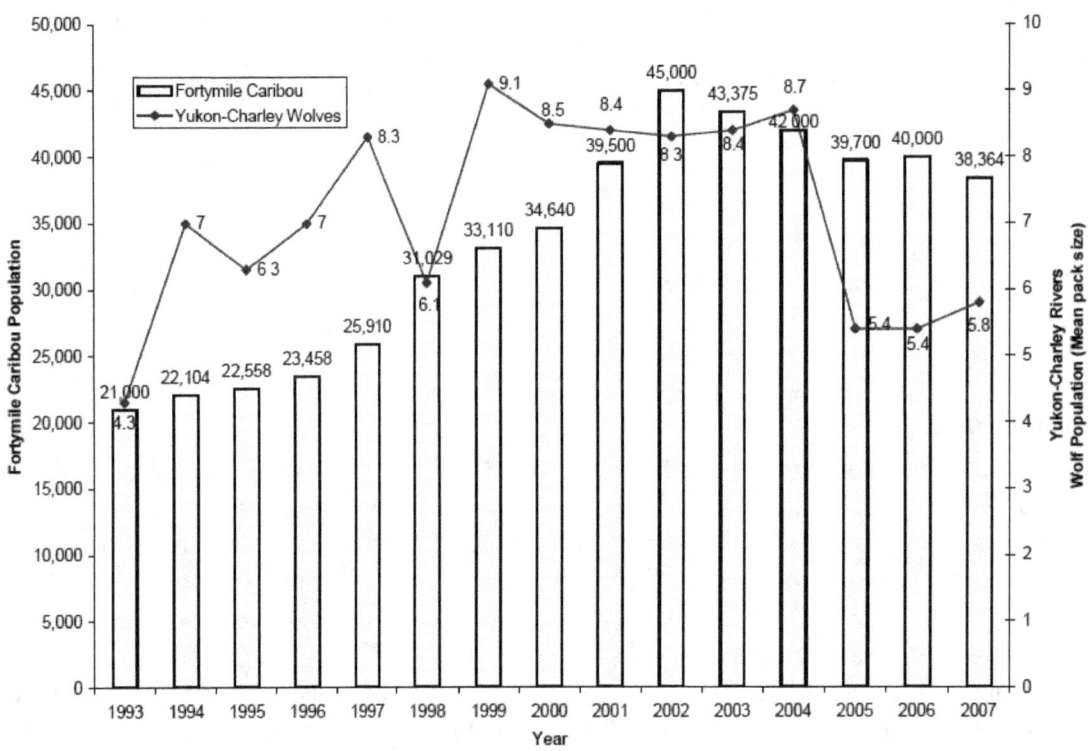

Figure 14. Trend in population change for the Fortymile Caribou Herd (trend in photo census counts) and wolves (in mean pack size) in Yukon-Charley Rivers National Preserve, Alaska, 1993 – 2007.

Natality

Pup production and survival to fall is illustrated in Figure 15. The counts of pups are from September - November of each year when the pups are still small enough to distinguish from adults from an airplane. Likely there are more pups born in May and some pup mortality occurs between May and September, so these are minimum counts. The cause of the drop in pup production and/or survival in 2004 and 2005 is unknown but correlates well with the overall drop in population size from 2004 to 2006 (Figures 11, 12, 13 & 14).

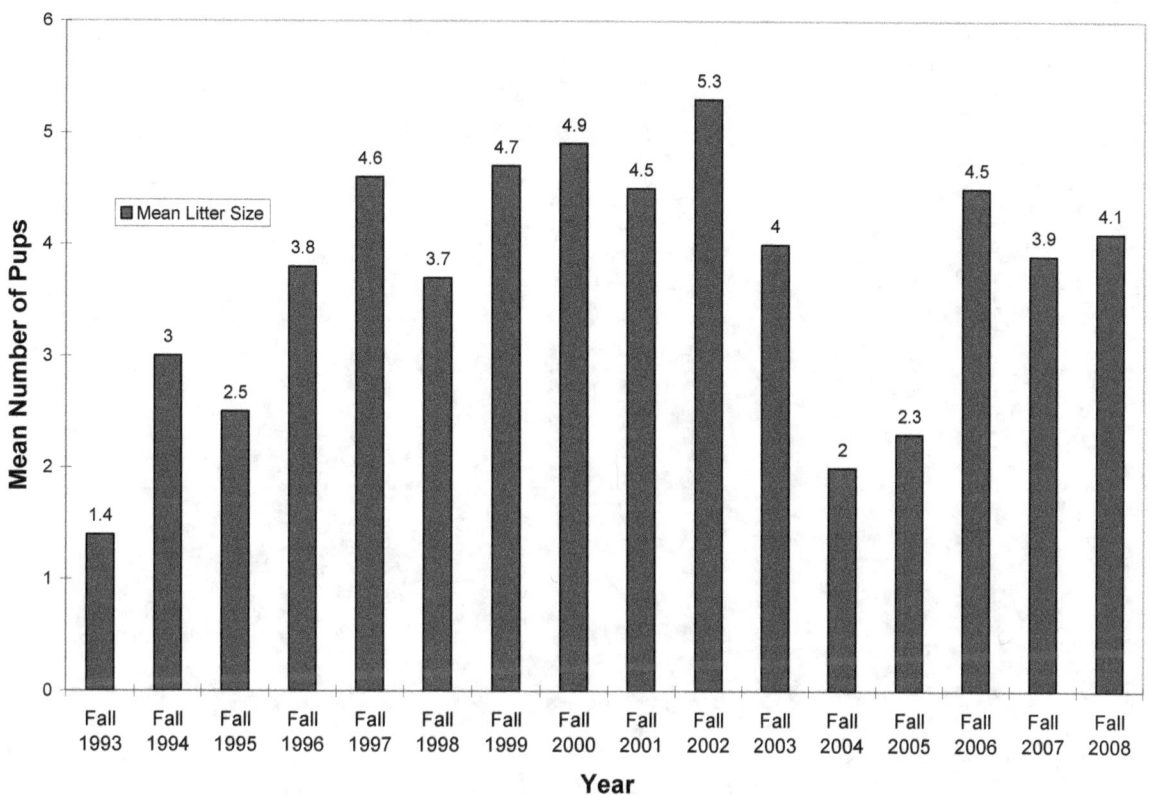

Figure 15 – Trend in Pup production and survival to fall (September/October mean litter sizes).

Mortality

All preserve packs travel outside the boundaries of YUCH, many extensively (Figure 2 - 6). As a result, regulations regarding wolf management outside YUCH's boundary affect the entire wolf population utilizing Preserve lands. This idea is well illustrated by The Alaska Board of Game's series of decisions to conduct wolf control up against most of YUCH's boundary south of the Yukon River (Figure 2 – 6, 9). However, winters 2006-07 and 2007-08 had poor conditions for snow tracking wolves, resulting in very few wolves being killed in the Fortymile Control efforts (58 in 2005-06, 13 in 2006–07, and 27 in 2007-08) far below the goal of reducing the entire population to somewhere between 88 - 103 wolves.

The situation changed some last winter (2008-09) where good snow tracking conditions existed for much of the area resulting in 48 wolves being shot from permitted fixed-wing airplanes. Furthermore, ADF&G decided to shoot wolves from helicopters March 14 – 19, 2009 throughout the Upper Yukon Tanana Predator Control Area (UYTPC), excluding YUCH. 84 wolves were shot from a helicopter in this portion of the control effort, however none of the killed wolves were from radiocollared packs that utilize YUCH lands (Figure 16). ADF&G estimates that approximately 66 wolves (average of previous years) will have been harvested by conventional hunting and trapping in the UYTPCA. This adds up to 198 wolves estimated to have been killed within UYTPCA for the 2008-09 season.

Figure 16. Map of the location and number of wolves killed by ADF&G shooting from a helicopter. No wolves from radio collared packs utilizing YUCH lands were known to have been killed via this method. Map was created and provided to NPS courtesy of ADF&G, Fairbanks, March 25, 2009.

Fates of a sample of 123 radiocollared wolves (from the beginning of the project in 1993) is illustrated in Figure 17. Although the sample of collared wolves is not representative of the population, they do give a good idea of what happens to most wolves in the Yuch population. About 20% are trapped or shot within the preserve boundary (or near it). The hunting season was extended in 2008 and now runs from August 10 – May 31 with a bag limit of 5 wolves south of the Yukon, and 10 wolves north of the Yukon (no limit for trapping). Even with these liberal regulations few wolves are harvested in or near YUCH most winters. Based on ADF&G sealing records, human harvest of wolves from within the preserve (via conventional trapping and hunting methods) has averaged about 7 wolves per year over the past 20 years (roughly 15% of the wolf population on average) (Figure 18) and has had little impact on YUCH's wolf population.

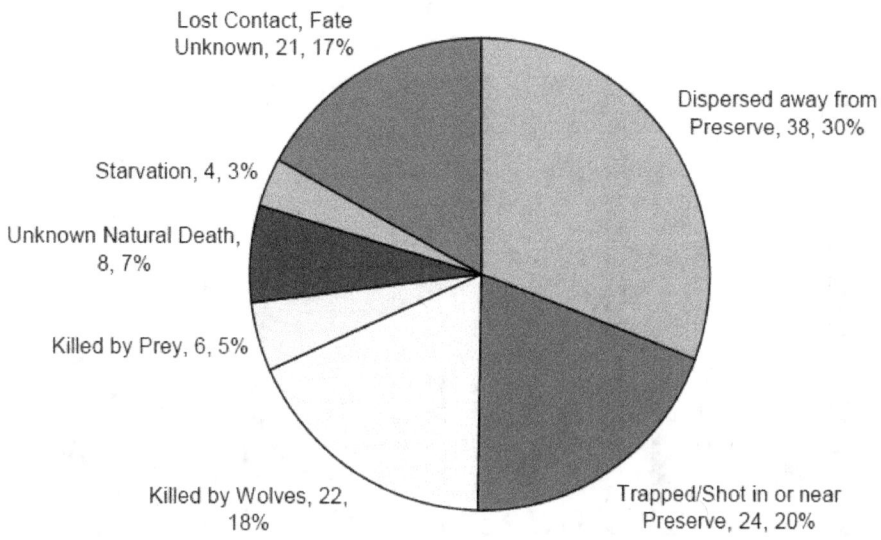

Fates of 123 Collared Wolves From Yukon Charley Rivers National Preserve
As of June 2009

Lost Contact, Fate Unknown, 21, 17%

Dispersed away from Preserve, 38, 30%

Starvation, 4, 3%

Unknown Natural Death, 8, 7%

Killed by Prey, 6, 5%

Killed by Wolves, 22, 18%

Trapped/Shot in or near Preserve, 24, 20%

Figure 17. Fates of collared wolves in and around YUCH, 1993 – 2009.

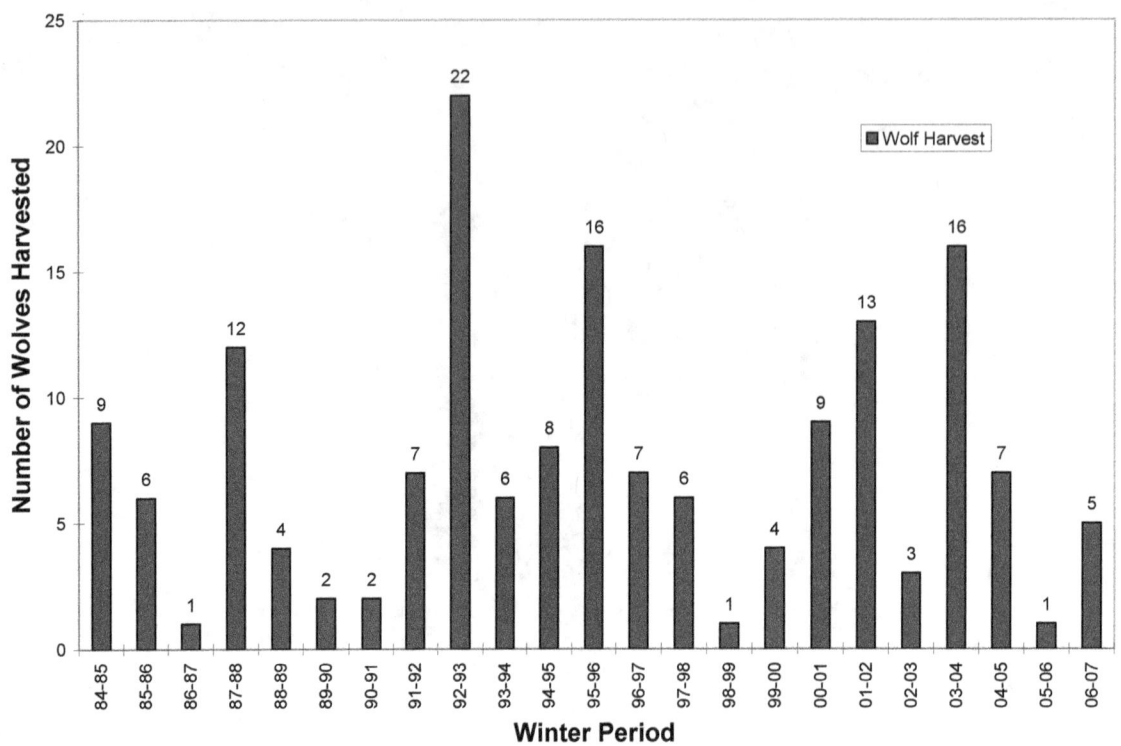

Figure 18. Harvest of wolves within and around YUCH, 1984 - 2007. From ADF&G wolf sealing records. Data not yet available from ADF&G for 2007-08 or 2008-09.

Genetics

Blood and /or tissue samples (cheek swabs and hair roots) are collected from all captured wolves for genetic analysis from both YUCH and Denali National Park and Preserve (Denali). Unique samples were collected from over150 individual wolves from both parks. Microsatellite data taken from the DNA extracted from these samples will be analyzed to assess the baseline levels of genetic variation in each wolf population and to determine the consistency of pack lineages.

Plans for Coming Year

In November 2009 and February 2010, we plan to capture more wolves to maintain 2 or 3 collars in each pack, and search for (and hopefully catch) wolves in any new or uncollared packs using Preserve lands. During this same time frame we will also be radiotracking the collared wolves from aircraft to get accurate pack counts for fall and spring population estimates. During Spring and Fall of each biological year the wolves will be radiotracked 5 – 10 times to generate biannual population estimates and estimate pup production and survival.

Literature Cited

Burch, J. W. 2002. Ecology and demography of wolves in Yukon-Charley Rivers National Preserve, Alaska. NPS Technical Report NPS/AR/NRTR-2001/41. 72pp.

Burch, J. W. 2006. Annual report on vital signs monitoring of distribution and abundance of wolves in Yukon-Charley Rivers National Preserve. Central Alaska Network, March 2006. NPS Fairbanks.14pp.

Burch, J. W. 2007. Annual report on vital signs monitoring of distribution and abundance of wolves in Yukon-Charley Rivers National Preserve. Central Alaska Network. NPS Fairbanks. 15pp.

Burch, J. W. 2008. Annual report on vital signs monitoring of wolf (*Canis lupus*) distribution and abundance in Yukon-Charley Rivers National Preserve, Central Alaska Network: 2008 report. Natural Resource Technical Report NPS/CAKN/NRTR—2008/149. National Park Service, Fort Collins, Colorado.

Burch, J. W., L. G. Adams, E. H. Follmann, and E. A. Rexstad. 2005. Evaluation of wolf density estimation from radiotelemetry data. Wildlife Society Bulletin 33(4):1225-1236

Fuller, T. K., L. D. Mech, and J. F. Cochrane. 2003. Wolf population dynamics. Pp. 161-191 *In* Mech, L.D., and L. Boitani, eds., Wolves: Behavior, Ecology, and Conservation. University of Chicago Press. 448 pp.

Mech L. D., L. G. Adams, T. J. Meier, J. W. Burch, B. W. Dale. 1998. The wolves of Denali. University of Minnesota Press, Minneapolis, Minnesota.

Mech, L. D., and S. M. Barber. 2002. A critique of wildlife radio-tracking and its use in National Parks. A report to the U. S. National Park Service.

Mech, L. D., and R. O. Peterson. 2003. Wolf-prey relations. Pp. 131-160 *In* Mech, L.D., and L. Boitani, eds., Wolves: Behavior, Ecology, and Conservation. University of Chicago Press. 448 pp.

Miller, B., B. Dugelby, D. Foreman, C. Martinez del Rio, R. Noss, M. Phillips, R. Reading, M. E. Soule', J. Terborgh, and L. Willcox. 2001. The importance of large carnivores to health ecosystems. Endangered species Update 18: 202-210.

National Park Service, 2001. Denali National Park and Preserve subsistence management plan. National Park Service, Denali Park, Alaska.

Ripple, W. J., and R. L. Beschta. 2003. Wolf reintroduction, predation risk, and cottonwood recovery in Yellowstone National Park. Forest Ecology and Management 184: 299-313.

Valkenburg P., D. G. Kelleyhouse, J. L. Davis, and J. M. Ver Hoef. 1994. Case history of the Fortymile caribou herd, 1920-1990. Rangifer 14: 11-22.

White, G.C. and R. A. Garrott. 1990. Analysis of wildlife radio-tracking data. Academic Press, San Diego, California.

Worton, B. J. 1989. Kernel methods for estimating the utilization distribution in home-range studies. Ecology 70:164-168.

NPS 191/100168, July 2009